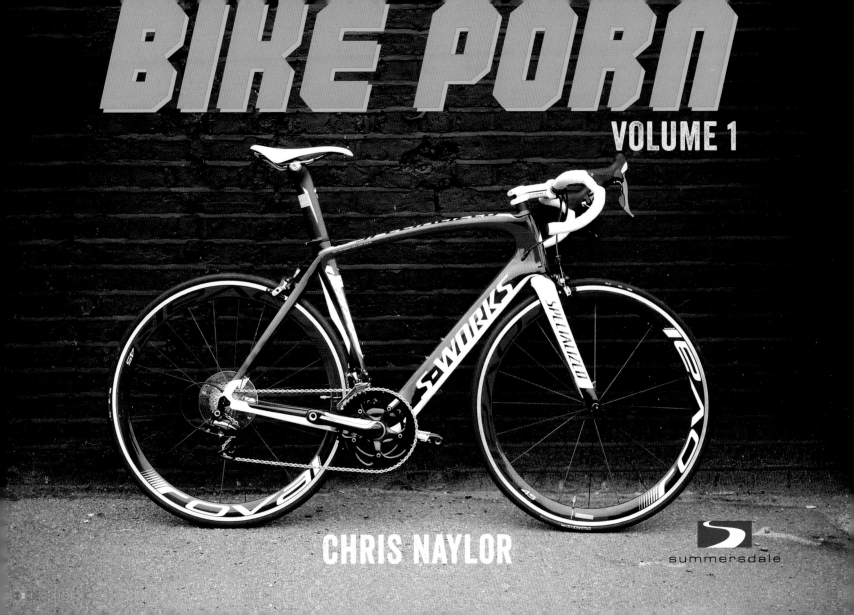

BIKE PORN

VOLUME 1

CHRIS NAYLOR

summersdale

BIKE PORN

Summersdale Publishers Ltd
46 West Street
Chichester
West Sussex
PO19 1RP
UK

www.summersdale.com

Printed and bound in China

ISBN: 978-1-84953-481-9

Substantial discounts on bulk quantities of Summersdale books are available to corporations, professional associations and other organisations. For details contact Nicky Douglas by telephone: +44 (0) 1243 756902, fax: +44 (0) 1243 786300 or email: nicky@summersdale.com.

INTRODUCTION

A BIKE IS ALWAYS MORE THAN THE SUM OF ITS PHYSICAL PARTS. BUT WHEN THOSE PARTS HAVE BEEN STYLED, SHAPED AND CRAFTED TO PERFECTION IT'S HARD NOT TO GET EXCITED. WHEN FORM AND FUNCTION COME TOGETHER BEAUTIFULLY IN THE SMOOTH CURVE OF A HANDLEBAR OR THE LINES OF A SLEEK, SLENDER FRAME EVEN THE UNTRAINED EYE GETS A LITTLE WIDER. THIS BOOK IS A CELEBRATION OF THE BICYCLE AS AN AESTHETICALLY PLEASING OBJECT — AND THE PASSION FOR DESIGN AND THE LOVE OF DETAIL THAT HAS GONE INTO CREATING THE CLASSIC AND CONTEMPORARY MACHINES FEATURED — MADE ALL THE MORE SEXY BY THE FACT THAT BIKES ARE NOT JUST GOOD-LOOKING, THEY'RE INTELLIGENT TOO. SO SIT BACK, RELAX AND PREPARE TO CATCH AN EYEFUL.

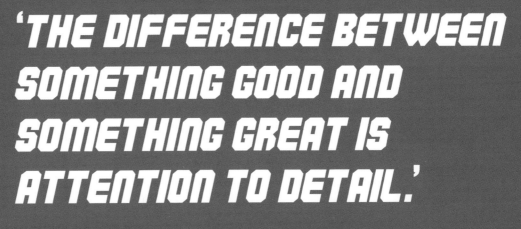

'THE DIFFERENCE BETWEEN SOMETHING GOOD AND SOMETHING GREAT IS ATTENTION TO DETAIL.'

CHUCK SWINDOLL

CINELLI MASH CNC STEM PISTA

'BEAUTY IS IN THE EYE OF THE BEHOLDER.'

MARGARET WOLFE HUNGERFORD

S-WORKS VENGE (CUSTOM BUILD)

'YOU DON'T HAVE TO GO FAST;
YOU JUST HAVE TO GO.'

ANONYMOUS

'IT'S THE LITTLE DETAILS THAT ARE VITAL. LITTLE THINGS MAKE BIG THINGS HAPPEN...'

JOHN WOODEN

HOLDSWORTH PROFESSIONAL

'*FREEDOM LIES IN BEING BOLD.*'

ROBERT FROST

COLOSSI LOW PRO

'THINK OF BICYCLES AS RIDEABLE ART THAT CAN JUST ABOUT SAVE THE WORLD.'

GRANT PETERSON

FORME FLASH

'FORM AND FUNCTION
SHOULD BE ONE...'

FRANK LLOYD WRIGHT

CAMPAGNOLO ATHENA DRIVETRAIN

'SPEED, IT SEEMS TO ME, PROVIDES THE ONE GENUINELY MODERN PLEASURE.'

ALDOUS HUXLEY

'FASHION FADES, ONLY
STYLE REMAINS THE SAME.'

COCO CHANEL

SCOTT CR1

'THE WORLD LIES RIGHT BEYOND THE HANDLEBARS OF ANY BICYCLE THAT I HAPPEN TO BE ON...'

DANIEL BEHRMAN

LOOK AL264 TRACK

'IT IS QUALITY RATHER THAN QUANTITY THAT MATTERS.'

SENECA THE YOUNGER

'BICYCLES MAY CHANGE, BUT CYCLING IS TIMELESS.'

ZAPATA ESPINOZA

FOFFA PRIMA

'THE OPEN ROAD IS A BECKONING...
A PLACE WHERE A MAN CAN LOSE
HIMSELF.'

WILLIAM LEAST HEAT-MOON

'TO POSSESS A BICYCLE IS TO BE ABLE FIRST TO LOOK AT IT, THEN TO TOUCH IT.'

JEAN-PAUL SARTRE

MERIDA WARP TT

'WHAT I DREAM OF IS AN ART OF BALANCE...'

HENRI MATISSE

MODA STRETTO

'RICHES DO NOT CONSIST IN THE POSSESSION OF TREASURES, BUT IN THE USE MADE OF THEM.'

NAPOLEON BONAPARTE

'THE BICYCLE IS THE NOBLEST INVENTION OF MANKIND.'

WILLIAM SAROYAN

CAMPAGNOLO BOTTECCHIA EQUIPE

'SIMPLICITY IS THE OUTCOME OF TECHNICAL SUBTLETY...'

FREDERIC WILLIAM MAITLAND

LOOK 695 AERO

'THE BICYCLE CAN BE USED IN SO MANY WAYS, AND APPROACHES PERFECTION IN EACH USE.'

BILL STRICKLAND

CINELLI LASER TRACK

'**THE FINEST MODE OF TRANSPORT KNOWN TO MAN.**'

ADAM HART-DAVIS

BAUM TURANTI

'IT IS THE UNKNOWN AROUND THE CORNER THAT TURNS MY WHEELS.'

HEINZ STÜCKE

'CYCLE TRACKS WILL ABOUND IN UTOPIA...'

H. G. WELLS

BMC TRACK MACHINE

'TRULY ELEGANT DESIGN INCORPORATES TOP-NOTCH FUNCTIONALITY INTO A SIMPLE, UNCLUTTERED FORM.'

DAVID LEWIS

COLNAGO MEXICO SUPER PANTOGRAFATA

'MELANCHOLY IS INCOMPATIBLE WITH BICYCLING.'

JAMES E. STARRS

AVENUE XS 1000

'CYCLING IS JUST LIKE CHURCH: MANY ATTEND, BUT FEW UNDERSTAND.'

JIM BURLANT

'THE BICYCLE HAS A SOUL... IT WILL GIVE YOU EMOTIONS THAT YOU WILL NEVER FORGET.'

MARIO CIPOLLINI

CLAUD BUTLER TT 01

'TRULY, THE BICYCLE IS THE MOST INFLUENTIAL PIECE OF PRODUCT DESIGN EVER.'

HUGH PEARMAN

RIDLEY HELIUM SL

'THE BICYCLE IS THE MOST
CIVILISED CONVEYANCE
KNOWN TO MAN.'

IRIS MURDOCH

KINFOLK BY RAIZIN

'A GOOD STYLE MUST HAVE AN AIR OF NOVELTY, AT THE SAME TIME CONCEALING ITS ART.'

ARISTOTLE

RADIOSHACK-NISSAN-TREK TEAM BIKE

'BICYCLING IS THE NEAREST
APPROXIMATION I KNOW TO
THE FLIGHT OF BIRDS.'

LOUIS J. HELLE, JR

'A MAN WHO WORKS WITH
HIS HANDS AND HIS BRAIN
AND HIS HEART IS AN ARTIST.'

LOUIS NIZER

BISHOP NIKKO DOWNTUBE LUG FINISHED

'BICYCLES HAVE NO WALLS.'

PAUL CORNISH

S-WORKS SHIV TT

'THE BEST RIDES ARE THE ONES WHERE YOU BITE OFF MUCH MORE THAN YOU CAN CHEW, AND LIVE THROUGH IT.'

DOUG BRADBURY

BIANCHI PISTA CONCEPT

'TO PROTRACT A GREAT
DESIGN IS OFTEN TO RUIN IT.'

MIGUEL DE CERVANTES

EDDY MERCKX CORSA

‘BE BOLD WHEN OTHERS ARE SCARED.’

THOMAS J. POWELL

PARLEE Z5i

'IT NEVER GETS EASIER, YOU JUST GO FASTER.'

'TO GET TO THE FINISH LINE,
YOU'LL HAVE TO TRY LOTS
OF DIFFERENT PATHS.'

AMBY BURFOOT

COLNAGO PISTA

'BE AT ONE WITH THE UNIVERSE. IF YOU CAN'T DO THAT, AT LEAST BE AT ONE WITH YOUR BIKE.'

LENNARD ZINN

CHARGE PLUG (RED BULL MINI DROME EDITION)

'WHY REINVENT THE WHEEL WHEN YOU CAN TIGHTEN THE SPOKES?'

ANONYMOUS

DT SWISS ENVE 3.4 CUSTOM

'THE DIFFERENCE BETWEEN THE IMPOSSIBLE AND THE POSSIBLE LIES IN A MAN'S DETERMINATION.'

TOMMY LASORDA

'**SIMPLICITY IS THE ULTIMATE SOPHISTICATION...**'

WILLIAM GADDIS

DE ROSA PROFESSIONAL SLX

'LIFE MAY NOT BE ABOUT YOUR BIKE, BUT IT SURE CAN HELP YOU GET THROUGH IT.'

ANONYMOUS

FORME ATT CARBON

'THE GOAL ISN'T TO LIVE FOREVER, THE GOAL IS TO CREATE SOMETHING THAT WILL.'

CHUCK PALAHNIUK

COOPER SPA

'THE BICYCLE IS ERGONOMICALLY TAILORED TO THE HUMAN FORM AND PSYCHE...'

BORIN VAN LOON

BAUM RISTRETTO

'IF YOU AREN'T GOING ALL THE WAY, WHY GO AT ALL?'

JOE NAMATH

'GRACE IS THE BEAUTY OF
FORM UNDER THE INFLUENCE
OF FREEDOM...'

FRIEDRICH SCHILLER

NEIL PRYDE ALIZE

'A BICYCLE RIDE AROUND THE WORLD BEGINS WITH A SINGLE PEDAL STROKE.'

SCOTT STOLL

PINARELLO DOGMA 60.1

'BICYCLES ARE ALMOST
AS GOOD AS GUITARS FOR
MEETING GIRLS.'

BOB WEIR

BISHOP (KHALIL'S FIXED GEAR)

'A BICYCLE HIDES NOTHING AND THREATENS NOTHING. IT IS WHAT IT DOES, ITS FORM IS ITS FUNCTION.'

STEWART PARKER

STEVENS COMET SL 5.0

'NOTHING COMPARES TO THE SIMPLE PLEASURE OF A BIKE RIDE.'

JOHN F. KENNEDY

FACTORY FIVE FS PISTA

'ONLY THE BICYCLE
REMAINS PURE IN HEART.'

IRIS MURDOCH

BLUE LUG CUSTOM PANASONIC

'RIDE AS MUCH OR AS LITTLE, OR AS LONG OR AS SHORT AS YOU FEEL. BUT RIDE.'

EDDY MERCKX

'THE CYCLIST IS A MAN HALF MADE OF FLESH AND HALF OF STEEL THAT ONLY OUR CENTURY OF SCIENCE AND IRON COULD HAVE SPAWNED.'

LOUIS BAUDRY DE SAUNIER

DEMON FRAMEWORKS CUSTOM BUILD

'KNOW YOUR LIMITS, BUT NEVER ACCEPT THEM.'

ANONYMOUS

BMC IMPEC

'SOMETIMES YOU HAVE TO TAKE THE BULL BY THE HORNS.'

PROVERB

INDEPENDENT FABRICATIONS PLANET X

'BE BOLD, BE BOLD, AND EVERYWHERE BE BOLD.'

EDMUND SPENSER

STRADALLI TREBISACCE RED-PRO

'AS LONG AS I'M RIDING A BIKE, I KNOW I'M THE LUCKIEST GUY IN THE WORLD.'

MARK CAVENDISH

S-WORKS + MCLAREN VENGE

'DARE TO BE DIFFERENT.'

ANONYMOUS

PEGORETTI FRAMES

'BICYCLING IS A BIG PART OF THE FUTURE. IT HAS TO BE.'

BILL NYE

'YOUR BIKE IS DISCOVERY;
YOUR BIKE IS FREEDOM.'

DOUG DONALDSON

ACKNOWLEDGEMENTS

FIRST AND FOREMOST, THANKS GO TO ALL OF THE PHOTOGRAPHERS, BIKE COMPANIES AND BIKE OWNERS WHO HAVE CONTRIBUTED TO THIS BOOK. SPECIAL THANKS TO PHOTO RESEARCHER LISA DULSON FOR AN EXCELLENT JOB AND TO ALEXA BALL FOR ASSISTANCE WITH THE TEXT.

PHOTO CREDITS

CALLING ALL BIKE PORN ENTHUSIASTS...

DO YOU HAVE AN EYE FOR A HEAVENLY HEADSET OR A SHAPELY SADDLE? IF SO, WE'D LIKE TO HEAR FROM YOU!
SEND IN YOUR OWN SHOTS OF SEXY BIKES AND BIKE PARTS TO BE IN WITH A CHANCE OF
FEATURING IN THE NEXT INSTALMENT OF BIKE PORN.

MAIL TO:

AUNTIE@SUMMERSDALE.COM

IF YOU'RE INTERESTED IN FINDING OUT MORE ABOUT OUR BOOKS,
FIND US ON FACEBOOK AT SUMMERSDALE PUBLISHERS
AND FOLLOW US ON TWITTER AT @SUMMERSDALE.

WWW.SUMMERSDALE.COM